YOU ARE THE BEST

DAD

a Daughter Could Have

ISBN: 978-1-68088-218-6

▉ and Blue Mountain Press are registered in U.S. Patent and Trademark Office. Certain trademarks are used under license.

Printed in China.
First Printing: 2018

♳ This book is printed on recycled paper.

This book is printed on paper that has been specially produced to be acid free (neutral pH) and contains no groundwood or unbleached pulp. It conforms with the requirements of the American National Standards Institute, Inc., so as to ensure that this book will last and be enjoyed by future generations.

Blue Mountain Arts, Inc.

P.O. Box 4549, Boulder, Colorado 80306

YOU ARE THE BEST

DAD

a Daughter Could Have

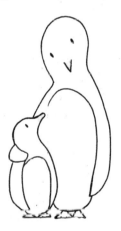

JENNY KEMPE

Blue Mountain Press™
Boulder, Colorado

Thank you for coming
home with nice surprises...

for arranging trips
and special outings...

...and for our time together,
just you and me.

You have always believed in me...

...never saying that I
aim too high or my ideas
are far-fetched.

You have given me rides to wherever I needed to go...

been my biggest fan...

...and come to my aid
countless times.

You have supported me, always.

Thank you for all the fun...

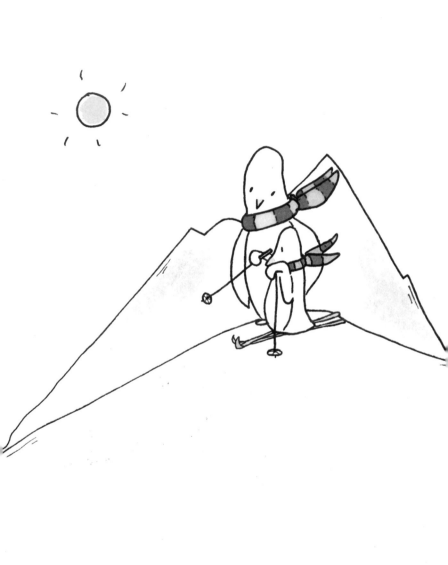

for teaching me new skills...

...and for doing the
same trick
over and over
and over and over
and over and over
again.

Thank you for encouraging
me to be brave...

for carrying me
when I got tired...

...and for protecting me.

More than anything,
thank you for allowing me
to grow up and become my
own person...

for trusting me to work
things out for myself...

...and for encouraging me
to go out and find
my own path.

You will always be
my dad and my
biggest hero.

I love you!